Seed, Flower, Fruit: From the Kingdom of Heaven to the Supreme Being

David Kantor

Urantia Book Films Press
Lakewood, Colorado

Quotations taken from The Urantia Book are from the public domain Standard
Reference Text published by Uversa Press, a service of The Urantia Book
Fellowship. The views expressed herein are solely those of the author and do
not necessarily represent the views of The Urantia Book Fellowship or any other
reader organization or publisher.

DEDICATION

Dedicated to those farseeing and forward-looking men and women of spiritual insight who will dare to construct a new and appealing philosophy of living out of the enlarged and exquisitely integrated modern concepts of cosmic truth, universe beauty, and divine goodness; the new teachers of Jesus' religion who will be exclusively devoted to the spiritual regeneration of men and women; the spirit-born souls who will quickly supply the leadership and inspiration requisite for the social, moral, economic, and political reorganization of the world.
—The Urantia Book, 2:7.10, 195:9.4

TABLE OF CONTENTS

PREFACE

This book provides a simplified paradigm for gaining insight into some of The Urantia Book's cosmological complexities. It is written with the assumption that you have formed some useful concepts about the Kingdom in the course of your reading of The Urantia Book, as well as something of Supremacy.

Two major themes, the Supreme Being and the Kingdom of Heaven, constitute primary structural elements of The Urantia Book's revelation of our relationship with God. These themes relate to our spiritual growth as individuals in the Kingdom, and the maturation of our cosmic citizenship in the milieu of Supremacy.

In addition to providing a paradigm for simplified understanding of the revelation, embracing this motif makes it easier to construct relevant and simple as-you-pass-by sharing of The Urantia Book's hopeful message. A fascinating exploration of this conceptual framework awaits you in the pages ahead.

Note: Certain key terms used throughout this book such as "Supreme Being," "Kingdom," "Experiential Deity," carry specialized meanings within the cosmology of The Urantia Book. A concise Note on Terminology is provided in Appendix III.

Jesus, the Kingdom of Heaven, and the Supreme

The Urantia Book is famously sprawling. On the surface, its four major divisions, multiple topics and number of authors makes it seem like a collection of discrete mini-revelations or loosely related articles. But there are specific themes that run through the entire text, unifying its cosmology and message. What unifies them is not initially obvious.

The entire book culminates in Part IV, The Life and Teachings of Jesus. But this is much more than mere biography—it's the interpretive key to everything preceding it. The first three parts of the book provide the cosmological scaffolding—the "stage" on which the drama of divine sonship plays out. The fourth part reveals how that cosmic pattern becomes personal, experiential, and human. In that sense, Jesus is the translation of the divine universe into the language of human life—the lens through which all cosmic truths gain moral and spiritual reality.

The Kingdom of Heaven is Jesus' chosen metaphor for reality as it is lived in relationship with God. It's existential—a state of personal fellowship with the Father. It's ethical—a way of living love, truth, and service. And, it's evolutionary—a seed growing within individuals and civilizations. The Kingdom represents Jesus' disclosure of how finite creatures can live in harmony with divine will.

The Supreme Being takes that same living relationship and projects it outward into universe destiny. Where the Kingdom is the living fellowship of sons and daughters of God, the Supreme is the synthesis of all those lives—the total realization of the Father's will across creation.

In that sense, the Supreme is the cosmic outworking of Jesus' gospel of the Kingdom, the divine enterprise that Jesus personalized and made accessible. The Supreme is not a secondary theme in The Urantia Book, but rather the cosmic flowering of what Jesus planted.

In the fifth epochal revelation, no longer is the Kingdom just the rule of God in a person's heart or in a community of believers, but the evolutionary precursor to the integration of all finite reality into a single, experiential Deity—God the Supreme.

The Kingdom is the genesis, the Supreme is the consummation. Both are woven throughout the four parts of The Urantia Book, hidden threads that weave theology, cosmology, history and biography into a single tapestry. This is why readers who recognize these two themes can begin to appreciate The Urantia Book in its entirety—not as an anthology, but a unified narrative with a beginning, middle and fulfillment.

Jesus' teaching about the Kingdom revealed, in personal terms, the very values and processes that the Supreme represents at the cosmic level. The Kingdom is the seed; the Supreme Being the flowering; God the Supreme, the fruit.

THE KINGDOM: Men and Women committed to doing the Father's will.
THE SUPREME: The superadditive consequence of all finite creatures doing the Father's will.

THE KINGDOM: Truth, beauty, goodness lived out in love, mercy, and service.
THE SUPREME: The integration of all values of love, mercy, and service into experiential Deity.

THE KINGDOM: Existential unification of people in shared love and loyalty.
THE SUPREME: Experiential unification of all finite love and loyalty across races, worlds, and universes.

THE KINGDOM: Voluntary loyalty—we choose to enter the Kingdom by faith and choosing to do the Father's will.
THE SUPREME: Convergent actualization—every creature choice is integrated into Deity growth.

THE KINGDOM: Immediate, conscious experience of fellowship with God and others.
THE SUPREME: Unconscious cosmic integration of all finite relationships.

THE KINGDOM: Eternal life through sonship; personal survival secured by choosing the Kingdom.
THE SUPREME: The completed sovereignty of the finite universes; the "fruit" of all Kingdom choices woven into one Deity.

> *Jesus' Kingdom teaching is a revelation at the human-scale of the same reality the Supreme embodies at the cosmic scale. By choosing to live in the Kingdom, we help build the Supreme, the emerging soul of the universe. In the Supreme Being, Creator and creature are united in one Deity whose will is expressive of one divine personality.*
> *—The Urantia Book, 117:1.5*

EVERYONE NEEDS A STORY

In popular spirituality today, spiritual teachings are often viewed through a psychological and therapeutic lens. This is spirituality as therapy—inwardly comforting but cosmically thin. It is the essence of theistic existentialism. It reduces the cosmic horizon of Jesus' message to the interior life of the individual rather than the unfolding of a divine purpose across all creation. "Spirituality" becomes emotional well being and social harmony. It is spiritual awareness with no story to explain or direct it.

Every person lives inside a story. We construct our social identities out of the stories we tell ourselves about reality and the roles we imagine ourselves to be playing in those stories. A story may be consciously created or unconsciously inherited.

When the story resonates in the social environment, people have direction and hope. If the story collapses, people feel lost, anxious, or fragmented. Story is more than entertainment—it's the architecture of meaning. The Urantia Book says that when there's no viable story available, people will inevitably make one up for themselves—universe frames in which thought can be ordered. Communities and civilizations are held together by shared stories. The biblical story once gave the Western world a unifying framework: creation, fall, redemption, heaven or hell. It held families, nations, and institutions together for centuries. When shared stories weaken, societies fracture; populations splinter into tribes or ideological camps. Without a common story, conflict replaces cohesion. Shared story is the invisible glue of civilization.

But what happens when people no longer believe the story?

When the Christian story began to crumble under the weight of science and skepticism, it wasn't just a religious crisis—it was also a cultural one. It left many people feeling adrift: isolated in their personal struggles, distrustful of institutions, suspicious of anyone else's story.

If the old story has collapsed then the urgent task is to tell a more relevant one—a story big enough to encompass science, philosophy, and religion, strong enough to provide social coherence; personal enough to heal the wounds of a damaged heart, compelling enough to catalyze a spiritual renaissance.

Two Millennia,
Two Revelations

If we are to take seriously Jesus' first century directive to proclaim the Kingdom in our twenty-first century world, it may be helpful for our orientation to the changed context, to compare the two differing conceptual environments in which the message must have relevance.

From Oppression by Empire to
Confusion of Worldviews

THEN: People suffered under Roman domination and yearned for freedom.
NOW: People suffer under the domination of meaninglessness—an empire of conflicting worldviews, information overload, and moral relativism. The mind is colonized by noise.
RELEVANCE: The Urantia Book liberates the modern mind by restoring cosmic coherence and integration. It weaves science, philosophy, and religion into a single, rational, spiritual model of reality. It gives modern people a universe that is both intelligible and divine—a cosmos they can trust again.

From Legalism to
Mechanistic Materialism

THEN: Religion had hardened into rule-keeping and ritual.
NOW: Science and secularism have hardened into reductionism— seeing the universe as a machine and the mind as a biochemical inevitability.
RELEVANCE: The Urantia Book restores the universe as a living system of purpose and personality. It honors the achievements of science but re-spiritualizes cosmology. It reintroduces a personal God and intelligent design without superstition, bridging the gulf between faith and reason.

FROM RITUAL PURITY TO
PSYCHOLOGICAL FRAGMENTATION

THEN: People were united, sharing ritual, liturgy, and belief.
NOW: People are divided—living fragmented digital lives, alienated from nature and one another.
RELEVANCE: The Urantia Book redefines spiritual wholeness as integration of the self with higher reality. Its teaching of the Thought Adjuster, the soul, and the Supreme Being reveals a process of inner unification—the vitalization of personality through the conscious pursuit of divine values: truth, beauty, and goodness.

FROM FEAR OF JUDGMENT TO
FEAR OF INSIGNIFICANCE

THEN: People feared God's wrath.
NOW: People fear that they don't matter—that they are ephemeral evolutionary events in an indifferent universe.
RELEVANCE: The Urantia Book restores personal dignity and cosmic belonging. It teaches that every human personality is unique, eternal, and loved by the Universal Father. It transforms insignificance into mission: we are co-creators in the evolution of the Supreme.

FROM CULTURAL TRIBALISM TO
GLOBAL INTERDEPENDENCE

THEN: The message of the Kingdom called individuals to embrace the Fatherhood of God and the brotherhood of man.
NOW: The revelation of the Supreme calls humanity to transcend national loyalties and realize a planetary fellowship—a global family bound by shared spiritual destiny.
RELEVANCE: The Urantia Book provides a planetary cosmology—a spiritual framework for global unity. It places our earth within a vast family of worlds, helping modern civilization see itself as one evolving planetary culture under divine guidance. It calls for the maturation of planetary civilization—the attainment of the age of light and life.

FROM EXPECTATION OF A MESSIAH TO EXPECTATION OF TECHNOLOGY

THEN: People waited for a supernatural deliverer.
NOW: We wait for technology, AI, or transhumanism to "save" us—to end suffering or grant immortality.
RELEVANCE: The Urantia Book redirects salvation from technology to personal spiritual evolution. It teaches that human destiny unfolds through the growth of the soul, through conscious co-operation with spirit—not through external miracles or material mastery.

FROM RELIGIOUS PROVINCIALISM TO SPIRITUAL MULTICULTURALISM

THEN: Religion was tribal and national.
NOW: Religion is multi-cultural.
RELEVANCE: Humanity is encountering all religions at once—Christianity, Islam, Hinduism, Buddhism, and the secular philosophies—creating both confusion and opportunity. The Urantia Book provides a meta-revelation—a synthesis that honors all genuine religious experience while transcending their partial views. It reframes revelation as progressive and inclusive, leading toward a planetary faith in one Father and one family.

FROM ANCIENT MYTH TO SCIENTIFIC NIHILISM

THEN: People tried to explain everything through myth and miracle.
NOW: People try to explain reality using science and probability.
RELEVANCE: The Urantia Book reconciles mythic meaning with scientific accuracy. It preserves the poetic grandeur of ancient faith while aligning it with evolutionary cosmology and experiential truth—showing that faith and fact are complementary expressions of reality.

From Expectation of the Kingdom to the Actualization of the Supreme

THEN: Believers waited in anticipation for Jesus to return so they could live in the Kingdom they believed he would establish.

NOW: The Urantia Book reveals humanity's participation in God the Supreme—the collective growth of all finite beings into a unified divine expression.

RELEVANCE: It expands the gospel from personal salvation to cosmic cooperation. Humanity is invited not merely to be saved, but to participate in the universe's growth—to transform civilization through truth, love, and spiritual insight.

> "The kingdom of God is in the hearts of men, and
> when this kingdom becomes actual in the heart of
> every individual on a world, then God's rule has
> become actual on that planet; and this is the attained
> sovereignty of the Supreme Being."
> —The Urantia Book, 118:10.17

From the Kingdom of Heaven to Experiential Deity

It may be surmised from the foregoing that the fifth epochal revelation greatly expands the content of what goes into Kingdom proclamation. While the revelation of the Supreme is not a replacement for Jesus' original gospel of the Kingdom; it extends it to reveal the Kingdom's cosmic unfolding: the next movement of the symphony of finite evolution.

Personal relationships mature into cosmic fellowship.

JESUS TAUGHT: "The Kingdom of God is within you." He revealed the indwelling Spirit of the Father—that every person can live as a son or daughter of God.

THE SUPREME EXTENDS THIS: "The Supreme is actualizing through you." The Urantia Book reveals that this divine presence in each person also links all persons together in the living soul of creation—God the Supreme. What begins as personal sonship blossoms into universal kinship.

Individual salvation leads to redemption of the whole.

JESUS TAUGHT: Each soul can be reborn into spiritual life—rescued from fear, guilt, and isolation by an act of faith; a spiritual decision to trust the leading of the Father's love and will.

THE SUPREME EXTENDS THIS: Salvation becomes social and planetary. When individuals live as citizens of the Kingdom, their collective goodness shapes civilization itself. The Supreme embodies the redemption of creation—the unification of all finite experience into one divine consciousness. The inner transformation of persons becomes the outer transformation of the world.

Faith in the Father's love is faith in the growth of the universe

JESUS TAUGHT: Faith opens the heart to God's presence now—trust in the Father's goodness is the key to peace.

13

THE SUPREME EXTENDS THIS: Faith also affirms the destiny of the cosmos—that the universe is growing toward perfection through experience. This gives meaning to struggle and suffering: they are not random but formative, building the wisdom of the Supreme. Faith matures from personal trust to cosmic confidence.

Brotherhood and sisterhood constitute co-creatorship with God

JESUS TAUGHT: All who do the will of God are brothers and sisters in the Kingdom

THE SUPREME EXTENDS THIS: Those same brothers and sisters are also co-creators in God's unfolding. Loving service is not just moral duty; it is the mechanism by which the Supreme grows. Community becomes a laboratory of divinity.

PRESENT SPIRITUAL EXPERIENCE IS ETERNAL COSMIC DESTINY

JESUS TAUGHT: Eternal life begins now; the soul that knows God need not wait to cross the portal of death.

THE SUPREME EXTENDS THIS: That eternal life continues as participation in the evolution of universes. Ascendant mortals will someday experience the completed Supreme—the very reality they helped to build through their choices in time. The personal becomes universal; the temporal becomes eternal.

Jesus' gospel of the Kingdom revealed the divine relationship—the Father and his children in loving fellowship. The Urantia Book's revelation of the Supreme reveals the divine process—the Father and his children working together to bring the universes to perfection. The first teaches communion; the second teaches co-creation. Together they describe the full arc of divine purpose from the birth of faith in a single heart to the consummation of wisdom in the soul of the cosmos.

> "The temporal relation of man to the Supreme is the
> foundation for cosmic morality, the universal sensitivity
> to, and acceptance of, duty. This is a morality which
> transcends the temporal sense of relative right and
> wrong; it is a morality directly predicated on the

self-conscious creature's appreciation of experiential obligation to experiential Deity. Mortal man and all other finite creatures are created out of the living potential of energy, mind, and spirit existent in the Supreme. It is upon the Supreme that the Adjuster-mortal ascender draws for the creation of the immortal and divine character of a finaliter. It is out of the very reality of the Supreme that the Adjuster, with the consent of the human will, weaves the patterns of the eternal nature of an ascending son of God."
—The Urantia Book, 117:4.8

The Gospel (Good News!) of the Supreme

The Urantia Book's portrayal of the nature of the Supreme (experiential Deity) is indeed good news for men and women in need of spiritual orientation and a motivating perspective on the purpose of the evolutionary process in which we find ourselves immersed.

The Urantia Book leads us from isolation to integration.

THE CONDITION: Modern men and women feel divided—inwardly fractured by competing loyalties, roles, and technologies. Psychology has replaced the soul with the self-image, and the result is fragmentation.

THE SUPREME'S ANSWER: The Supreme is the synthesis of all finite experience—the unifying consciousness of creation. As individuals integrate truth, beauty, and goodness in their lives, they mirror that universal integration. The teaching of the Supreme gives meaning to our struggle for wholeness: every sincere effort to unify the self in love and purpose contributes to the unification of the whole.

The Urantia Book leads us from stagnant meaninglessness to mobilizing purpose.

THE CONDITION: Science has given us mechanism without meaning; the universe seems vast, impersonal, and indifferent.

THE SUPREME'S ANSWER: The Supreme restores purpose to evolution. Creation is not random but cumulative—a divine project in which all experience matters. Human life gains dignity because every moral choice adds to the growth of God's own experiential reality. Our personal stories become threads in a cosmic tapestry still being woven.

THE URANTIA BOOK LEADS US FROM CYNICISM TO FAITH IN GROWTH.

THE CONDITION: Modern idealism has burned out. We no longer trust progress, institutions, or even goodness to prevail.
THE SUPREME'S ANSWER: Growth is sacred. The universe itself is learning—Deity is actualizing through experience. This gives realism to hope: even slow moral progress and painful lessons are cosmic education. Faith in the Supreme means faith in the eventual triumph of wisdom.

THE URANTIA BOOK LEADS US FROM PRIVATE SPIRITUALITY TO COOPERATIVE DESTINY.

THE CONDITION: Contemporary spirituality is often solitary—each person seeking enlightenment for themselves, disconnected from collective purpose.
THE SUPREME'S ANSWER: The Supreme transforms private religion into planetary co-creation. The divine grows through relationship—between persons, communities, and civilizations. Spiritual progress becomes a shared adventure. The Supreme evolves through us as we incorporate spiritual values in our interactions with others.

THE URANTIA BOOK LEADS US FROM ETHICAL RELATIVISM TO VALUE REALISM.

THE CONDITION: Modern moral confusion stems from the loss of any transcendent standard; "truth" feels like opinion.
THE SUPREME'S ANSWER: The values of truth, beauty, and goodness are universal and real. They are the ways the finite participates in the eternal. Through the Supreme, these values are personalized—they are the very character of the growing God of experience. To live by them is to align with the universe's creative direction.

18

The Urantia Book leads us from Cosmic loneliness to belonging.

THE CONDITION: We are hyper-connected electronically, yet existentially alone. We feel small—conscious specks in a silent cosmos.
THE SUPREME'S ANSWER: The Supreme reveals that no experience is isolated. Each life adds to the living soul of creation. We belong not only to humanity, but to a growing divine being who feels and remembers through us. Our choices echo eternally in the evolution of experiential Deity.

The Urantia Book leads us from passive belief to active partnership with God.

THE CONDITION: Many have lost interest in religion as a spectator activity—doctrines to accept, rituals to repeat.
THE SUPREME'S ANSWER: Religion becomes participatory. We are not merely believers but co-creators. To act in love, to discover truth, to beautify the world—these are ways of collaborating with the divine will. The Supreme invites us to see spiritual living as creative work, not mere obedience.

The Urantia Book leads us from the Kingdom within to the Supreme's Emergence.

Jesus revealed that the Kingdom of God lives within—the personal realization of divine sonship. The Urantia revelation extends that vision outward. As the Kingdom grows within individuals, the Supreme grows through all individuals together. What begins in the heart becomes civilization's destiny—the emergence of experiential Deity from human experience.

The revelation of the Supreme Being answers the modern crisis of fragmentation, nihilism, and disconnection. It restores to humanity a sense of participation in something larger, living, and loving—an exciting universe where growth is sacred, values are real, and every person contributes to the becoming of God.

THE PHILOSOPHIC ARC: FROM EXISTENTIALISM TO SUPREMACY

Christianity's loss of its supportive cosmology over the past few hundred years has led it into existentialism in both theology and in common belief. Existentialism asks, "How shall I live authentically in this moment?" The Kingdom/Supreme proclamation asks, "How shall I live cooperatively in the divine unfolding of the cosmos?" It is the same spiritual consciousness, extended outward in time—from personal being to collective becoming.

Our civilization, shaped by humanism, psychology, and secularism, tends to privatize spirituality—treating it as an individual coping mechanism rather than a collective cosmic vocation. Discovering the teleological dimension of Jesus' teachings (Supremacy) is essential to recognizing the cosmic context of his gospel of the Kingdom. It shows people that their daily moral and spiritual acts are not isolated gestures of meaning, but threads in the fabric of universe evolution.

THE KINGDOM AS COSMIC ORIENTATION

When Jesus said "The Kingdom of heaven is within you" and "at hand," he wasn't describing a place—he was describing a state of relationship. It is the moment when the human will aligns with the divine will.

To enter the Kingdom is to consent to the divine purpose; a personal decision to participate in divine reality. That consent empowers the individual soul to become a conscious participant in a greater process—the unfolding of the Supreme.

THE SUPREME AS THE COLLECTIVE CONSEQUENCE

Where the Kingdom is experienced, the Supreme is constructed. The Supreme is the accumulated synthesis of all finite creatures' experiences of doing the Father's will in time. Each act of living truthfully and lovingly adds a value-unit to the growing soul of the Supreme.

Thus to live in the Kingdom now is to build the Supreme forever. Every decision for truth or goodness, every act of proclamation that expands divine order in the world, becomes part of the finite expression of the Infinite's purpose.

> "The motivation of faith makes experiential the full realization of man's sonship with God, but action, completion of decisions, is essential to the evolutionary attainment of consciousness of progressive kinship with the cosmic actuality of the Supreme Being."
> —The Urantia Book, 110:6.17

From Kingdom/Supreme Synthesis to Global Transformation

The Kingdom religion of Jesus leads to the discovery and assimilation of values repercussing in the actualization of the Supreme in the theater of everyday life through the infusion of spiritual values into the material world.

Science and Technology

KINGDOM INSIGHT: Living in the Kingdom orients the mind toward truth, humility, and service. It cultivates intellectual honesty and ethical responsibility. A Kingdom-oriented scientist is less likely to distort data for fame or funding and more likely to pursue knowledge for the good of humanity.

SUPREME CONTEXT: Understanding that all finite experience contributes to the growing Supreme gives meaning to scientific work—it isn't just about discovery, but about weaving truth into the larger tapestry of reality. This motivates perseverance and fosters collaboration over competition.

Business and Economics

KINGDOM INSIGHT: Business becomes more than profit-seeking; it becomes stewardship. The Kingdom ideal pushes toward fairness, integrity, and treating employees and customers as ends, not means.

SUPREME CONTEXT: Recognizing that every choice has cosmic value encourages sustainable practices. A business decision isn't just local or temporal—it echoes in the growth of the Supreme. That perspective elevates responsibility for social impact, environmental balance, and long-term human flourishing.

KINGDOM INSIGHT: The Kingdom teaches that all people are children of the Father. This undermines tribalism, nationalism, and prejudice. It reframes conflicts not as us vs. them but as opportunities to serve and uplift.

SUPREME CONTEXT: The Supreme embodies the slow, painful synthesis of all human struggle into a higher unity. In times of turmoil, understanding this helps people see beyond immediate chaos. Social conflict itself becomes raw material for a higher integration, fostering patience, creativity, and resilience.

KINGDOM INSIGHT: Anchors the individual in faith, love, and hope. Even in crisis, there is inner stability because identity is rooted in the Father's will.

SUPREME CONTEXT: Gives assurance that no experience is wasted—everything contributes to the universe's teleological evolution. This prevents despair and helps people accept setbacks as part of a larger, meaningful process.

PERSONAL STABILITY IN TURMOIL

The Kingdom/Supreme synthesis offers both a personal compass and a cosmic horizon. That combination empowers people to work more honestly in science, more ethically in business, more cooperatively in politics, and more hopefully in a world of social upheaval.

Proclaiming the fifth epochal revelation's expanded understanding of the Kingdom illuminates the bridge linking personal realization (the Kingdom within) to universal realization (the Supreme without). To proclaim is to co-create. The universe advances not merely by divine fiat but through the cumulative actions of conscious beings. The Master's commission to proclaim has the same urgency today as when he issued the directive.

When Jesus said "Go, proclaim the Kingdom," he was effectively saying: Become agents of the universe's evolution; make divine reality visible on Earth. Proclaiming the Kingdom is mortal participation in divine creation.

An existential view explains things in terms of immediate experience and personal meaning—an awakening within something. A teleological view explains things in terms of their purpose, final cause, or ultimate goal—a movement toward something.

One turns inward to discover meaning; the other looks outward to discern purpose. Together they form the full circle of spiritual understanding—the presence of God within, and the purpose of God unfolding through time.

> "Joyful acceptance of cosmic citizenship—honest recognition of your progressive obligations to the Supreme Being, awareness of the interdependence of evolutionary man and evolving Deity: This is the birth of cosmic morality and the dawning realization of universal duty."
> —The Urantia Book, 110:3.10.4

THE SUPREME BEING AND THE KINGDOM OF HEAVEN

Growth in the Kingdom has to do with values we use to shape our relationships and make life decisions. Growth of the Supreme is the repercussion. Both stress partnership between the human and the divine. The "Kingdom" was a way to introduce a spiritualized vision in the first century. The "Supreme" is a way to universalize that same vision in a twenty-first century framework of cosmic philosophy.

Where the Kingdom is about entering into God's will now, the Supreme is about the universe-wide outcome of everyone entering into God's will over time. Growth in the Kingdom and growth in the Supreme are the essence of evolving cosmic citizenship.

Jesus revealed the personal nature of God—the Universal Father—and proclaimed the Kingdom of heaven as the living experience of doing the Father's will. The Supreme represents the finite universe's integration of all such creature experiences of choosing and doing God's will.

Jesus' teaching about the Kingdom (personal and social realization of God's will) becomes the philosophical and religious seed that blossoms into The Urantia Book's story of the Supreme (cosmic realization of God's will). Jesus' dual nature—both human and divine—exemplifies the very finite-infinite blending that the Supreme embodies on a cosmic scale.

Think of the Kingdom as a garden patch within a large field. It is watered by faith, cultivated by love. The Supreme is like the entire ecosystem of the field—every plant, every cycle, every harvest, gathered into a unified whole.

Jesus localized the Father's rule in human lives; the Supreme universalizes it into cosmic destiny. What Jesus planted in mortal history, the Supreme harvests into eternal destiny.

What this means is that our moral struggles, our creative acts, our loyalty to truth, our small victories in faith—they don't vanish. They are woven into the very growth of God the Supreme and are direct contributions to the cosmic storehouse of values that will be available for finaliter ministry in the outer space levels. Knowing this makes every decision significant: our lives literally matter to Deity and the future evolution of the cosmos. The meaning of my life is not just "me and God," but "me, God, and the destiny of the universe together."

When we face hardships and difficult decisions, we're not just hanging on until we get to the mansion worlds. We are participating in the evolutionary growth of experiential Deity. No effort is ever wasted. Even small acts of loyalty and courage contribute to the qualitative growth of the Supreme. This teaching transforms ordinary struggle, service, and growth into participation in the very becoming of Deity. It ennobles the mundane living of daily life.

> "The universe procession of descending God-revealing Creators and ascending God-seeking creatures is revelatory of the Deity evolution of the Supreme, in whom both descenders and ascenders achieve mutuality of understanding, the discovery of eternal and universal brotherhood. The Supreme Being thus becomes the finite synthesis of the experience of the perfect-Creator cause, and the perfecting-creature response."
> —The Urantia Book, 117:1.2

Living in the Kingdom,
Living With the Supreme

Living with the Supreme is experienced unconsciously as growth through the psychic circles of mortal progression. (See Appendix I) The Urantia Book presents living in the Kingdom and ascent through the circles as integral complements of spiritual growth, personal maturation into spiritual wholeness. No longer does spiritual insight remain an existential property of subjective consciousness: it flows out through the individual into the material world where it can transform mortal culture.

Living in the Kingdom:
Manifesting the Will of God

ESSENCE: Doing the Father's will; experiencing sonship with God and brotherhood with others.

FOCUS: Personal loyalty, love, and service.

CONSCIOUSNESS: Directly felt in prayer, peace, joy, and fellowship.

MEASURE: Qualitative—not about external achievement but sincerity of choice and depth of relationship.

Living with the Supreme:
Ascending the Psychic Circles

ESSENCE: Cultivating levels of soul development that lead to higher levels of personality integration with cosmic reality.

FOCUS: Loyalty to the highest values derived from progressive living in the Kingdom.

CONSCIOUSNESS: Not always directly felt; progress is usually unconscious, though growth may be sensed.

MEASURE: Quantitative—seven circles of advancement leading to the first circle, then Adjuster fusion. (See Appendix I)

The Foundation of
Mortal Spiritual Maturity

Kingdom living is the method; psychic circles are the naturally progressing steps of attainment on the path toward destiny. Every act of love, loyalty, and faith in the Kingdom contributes to advancement through the circles. Entering the Kingdom (choosing God's will) corresponds to entering the circle ascent. Deepening Kingdom life (progressing in sonship and brotherhood) corresponds to moving inward through the circles.

Reaching spiritual maturity (fusion with the Adjuster) is the culmination of both—the perfected child of the Kingdom, standing ready for the universe ascent. Living in the Kingdom is the journey itself—the conscious way of life: trust, love, and service. The psychic circles are the mile-markers along the road—the cosmic measurement of how far integration with the Supreme has progressed. They describe the same pilgrimage: one speaks the language of Jesus' parables, the other the language of personality identity.

Each circle reflects a broader loyalty, until the soul defines itself not by self, tribe, or nation, but by loyalty to God's will as embodied in the welfare of the whole—the Supreme. It is the movement from self-interest to cosmic identification with the Supreme.

Progress through the Circles

Traversing the psychic circles marks progress in personality coordination and integration with the cosmos. Each circle represents a stage where one's motives, decisions, and identity are less fragmented and more attuned to the divine pattern. By the higher circles, the individual is no longer simply "behaving" according to cosmic values but actually thinking, feeling, and acting from a unified selfhood in partnership with the Adjuster and the Supreme. These are actual levels of functional attainment integrated into the decision making trends of the mortal mind.

THE GOSPEL (GOOD NEWS!) EXPANDED BY THE URANTIA BOOK

The Urantia Book maintains core continuity with Jesus' first century teaching. The heart of the message has not changed: The Fatherhood of God; The brotherhood and sisterhood of all people; the invitation to enter the Kingdom by choosing God's will. The Kingdom is present here and now. It is an experiential reality.

The gospel is still personal and relational at its core—no scientific advance can replace love, truth, and loyalty. Jesus' gospel of the Kingdom is the good news that God is our loving Father, that we are his children, and that all humanity is called to live in love, truth, and service under the divine rule of the spirit—beginning now and extending to eternity.

IN RELATION TO SCIENCE

Science has revealed the immensity of the universe—the Kingdom must be presented as cosmic in scope. Rather than competing with science, the Kingdom message should affirm that the laws of nature are the expression of an intelligent and benevolent Source.

THE GOSPEL TODAY: "The same God who rules the galaxies dwells within you as a loving Father."

IN RELATION TO PHILOSOPHY

Modern philosophy wrestles with meaning, value, and the problem of fragmentation. The Kingdom can be presented as the living unity of values—truth, beauty, and goodness actualized in human lives.

THE GOSPEL TODAY: "Life has direction and purpose because love, truth, and goodness are real, and your choices help weave them into the fabric of the universe."

In Relation to Religion

Humanity is now pluralistic, with many religions side by side. The Kingdom should be presented not as sectarian, but as a spiritual family transcending creeds.

THE GOSPEL TODAY: "All faiths that honor God's will belong to the same family—the Kingdom of heaven."

Integration with the Supreme

Jesus spoke in terms of Kingdom and family; today we can add the cosmic perspective: that our personal loyalty contributes to the growth of the Supreme Being.

THE GOSPEL TODAY: "Your personal faith not only saves your soul but helps the very universe grow into God." This does not replace Jesus' teaching but expands it to the scale of modern cosmology and revelation.

IN JESUS' TIME: "Kingdom"—useful but limited, adapted to his hearers.

UNDERLYING TRUTH: "Family"—the Fatherhood of God and the brotherhood of man.

REVELATORY EXPANSION: "Supreme Being"—the universal family integrated into a Deity personality.

The Implications

PROCLAIM: God is our loving Father, and we are His children.

INVITE: Choose the Father's will—that is entrance into the Kingdom.

AFFIRM: All who do so are brothers and sisters in one spiritual family.

EXPAND: The service we render; every choice we make for truth, loyalty, goodness, beauty; every assimilation of spiritual values into our lives—contribute to the quality of the universe's destiny in the Supreme.

ENCOURAGE: Live love, practice truth, create beauty—for these are the building blocks of the Kingdom and the very substance of God's evolving presence.

Today the gospel of the Kingdom is the proclamation that God is our Father, all people are one family, and every act of faith, love, truth, beauty, and goodness, not only transforms lives here but also contributes to the very growth of God in the time-space universe.

The Kingdom is where we choose to live with God; the Supreme is where all our choices become a living part of experiential Deity and live on forever. This is the great story in which we each play a part. Living in the Kingdom enhances personal spirituality. Living with the Supreme leads to engagement with evolutionary process.

> *"All soul-evolving humans are literally the evolutionary*
> *sons of God the Father and God the Mother, the*
> *Supreme Being."*
> —*The Urantia Book, 117:6.8*

PROCLAMATION IN THE
FIFTH EPOCH

We must start by establishing some context for ourselves, with understanding the contemporary human situation into which the revelation needs to be introduced.

MODERNITY'S PROBLEM: We gained science but lost meaning.
POSTMODERNITY'S PROBLEM: We exposed false certainties but lost hope in any shared story.
THE RESULT: People are hungry for purpose, belonging, and hope.

TRANSLATE THE KINGDOM MESSAGE
INTO TODAY'S TERMS

JESUS' TIME: "The Kingdom of heaven is at hand." Urgent, simple, revolutionary.
TODAY: We need equally direct language: "You are not a random evolutionary event in a cold universe. You are a child of a loving Father." "We are one human family, meant to grow together." "Your choices of truth, love, and goodness matter eternally—they help build the future of our world and the universe."

MAKE THE KINGDOM A NEW PARADIGM
OF CREATIVE RELIGIOUS LIVING

Not a religion to join, but a way of seeing reality; Life has meaning; Relationships matter eternally; The universe is unfinished—and we are invited to help God complete it. This reframes "salvation" from escaping hell to participating in the story of experiential Deity emerging in time.

FRAME IT AS LIBERATION FROM
POSTMODERN FRAGMENTATION

POSTMODERNISM SAYS: "There is no big story."
THE KINGDOM SAYS: "There is a big story—and you have a role to play in it."

POSTMODERNISM SAYS: "Values are relative."

THE KINGDOM SAYS: "Love, truth, and goodness are real—and your choices bring them to life." Postmodernism leaves us lonely and skeptical. The Kingdom invites us into family and destiny.

To move from abstraction to compelling message, we speak less about "integration of finite values into Deity" and more about family, belonging, destiny, and participation—a story that rescues us from postmodern fragmentation by giving us a hopeful, unifying paradigm.

Jesus was calling people to participate in an advancing spiritual civilization—one whose culmination lies not merely in human fulfillment but in the progressive realization of divine will within time, what we might call the temporal manifestation of the Supreme.

So when Jesus said "proclaim the Kingdom," he wasn't instructing us merely to preach or persuade—he was summoning us to become active participants in the actualization of divine purpose on Earth.

We can imagine a Jesus of today telling his followers:

- The Kingdom is here now, whenever you choose God's will.

- Every act of goodness and service helps shape the very future of the universe.

- You are not an inconsequential byproduct of evolution. You are children of a loving Father. Go and tell the world.

- We are one family, meant to live in love and truth.

- Every act of goodness and courage helps shape the future of the universe.

- This is the story that heals our age and gives your life eternal meaning.

- We live in an unfinished universe, alive with purpose and promise.

- Every person has a part to play in its great unfolding.

- You are a child of the Infinite Father, and your choices of truth, love, and beauty help shape the destiny of creation itself.

- The Kingdom of heaven is here, in every heart that chooses God's will, and together we are building the future of the Supreme—the living soul of the evolving cosmos.

This is the adventure of the ages: a universe becoming divine, and every life essential to its fulfillment.

> *"The absonite architects eventuate the plan; the Supreme Creators bring it into existence; the Supreme Being will consummate its fullness as it was time created by the Supreme Creators, and as it was space forecast by the Master Architects."*
> —The Urantia Book, 106:3.1

OUR CREATIVE PARTICIPATION AS CO-CREATORS OF DESTINY

If reality is indeed a divine unfolding in which the Kingdom and the Supreme are two dimensions of the same process, then conscious participation requires making them both part of our personal philosophy of life and service.

THE KINGDOM DIMENSION: PERSONAL CHOICE AND SPIRIT ALIGNMENT

INNER ORIENTATION: Choosing daily to center ourselves in faith, trust, and loyalty rather than fear or cynicism. This is "seeking first the Kingdom."

RELATIONSHIPS: Treating people with dignity and love—seeing them as fellow citizens of a higher reality, even when society is polarized or hostile.

MORAL COURAGE: Refusing to surrender to hatred, dishonesty, or despair, even when those forces dominate the headlines.

This is the personal, conscious part of our role: deciding to live as if the Kingdom were already real, even in turbulent times.

THE SUPREME DIMENSION: EXPERIENTIAL INTEGRATION

The Supreme represents the totalization of finite experience, the weaving of our choices into the fabric of evolving deity. In practice:

SERVICE BEYOND SELF: Engaging in efforts that lift others—whether in our family, community, or work. Every act of unselfish service adds to the strength of the Supreme.

CREATIVE CONTRIBUTION: Bringing our unique talents into play—art, teaching, healing, building, storytelling. Civilization may be turbulent, but the Supreme grows through creative labor.

ENDURANCE IN GROWTH: Understanding that progress is cumulative; even small advances in patience, cooperation, or justice help civilization's eventual renewal.

This is the cosmic, unconscious part of our role. Our choices ripple out into an evolving whole, whether we're aware of it or not.

Jesus revealed the Father as personal and loving. By living a life of perfect union with God, he embodied the principle of the Supreme—the experiential unification of finite and divine. His Kingdom message was therefore not just a spiritual ethic, but a window into the very process by which the Supreme is evolving.

Everyday Practices for the Interregnum

When civilization goes through periods of increased turbulence, men and women of spiritual insight must find ways to help with stabilization in their domains of influence. Here are a few suggestions which can be incorporated into practical habits in daily life:

CLARITY THROUGH PRAYER, AND WORSHIP: Anchor our minds daily in prayer, worship, meditation, or reflection, so we're not swept away by the news cycle.

HOPEFUL SPEECH: Speak words that uplift, not inflame—become a voice of stability and vision.

COMMUNITY TIES: Build and sustain circles of trust where mutual support and higher values can be lived.

RESILIENT WORK: Offer our crafts, trades, skills, or art not just as survival, but as contribution to a better collective story.

PATIENT WITNESS: Trust that even in breakdown, the Supreme is gathering the value of experience toward eventual synthesis.

SELFLESS SERVICE: Tend to the emotional, psychological, and spiritual needs of people we encounter in daily life wherever and whenever as may be appropriate.

This is how everyday choices—how we listen, work, forgive, and create—become the very substance of the universe's unfolding: the seed of the Kingdom has matured in our lives, leading to identity in the flowering of the Supreme. The final fruits of destiny await us.

"Having started out on the way of life everlasting, having accepted the assignment and received your orders to advance, do not fear the dangers of human forgetfulness and mortal inconstancy, do not be troubled with doubts of failure or by perplexing confusion, do not falter and question your status and standing, for in every dark hour, at every crossroad in the forward struggle, the Spirit of Truth will always speak, saying, "This is the way."
—The Urantia Book, 34:7.8

Appendix I:
The Psychic Circles
and Identity Formation

We can map the psychic circles in terms of progressive personality integration with the cosmos. The Urantia Book doesn't spell out all seven in detail, but it gives enough hints that we can speculate a bit and try to construct a coherent picture. A person's moral system reflects their ultimate concern—the reality they hold as most real and most worthy of devotion. The more one's ultimate concern aligns with the divine will and evolving unity of creation (the Supreme), the more one's identity becomes stable, real, and enduring; the farther along the circles ascent we find ourselves.

7th Circle—Awakening Self

PERSONALITY INTEGRATION: First moral awakenings; self sees a universe of right and wrong.
MORALITY FOCUS: Self—personal integrity, conscience, and responsibility.
COSMIC RESONANCE: The spark of cosmic citizenship: "I matter in a universe that has meaning."

6th Circle—Family & Tribe

PERSONALITY INTEGRATION: Living for others—loyalty, responsibility, sacrifice.
MORALITY FOCUS: Family and close group—relationships start to outweigh self-centeredness.
COSMIC RESONANCE: Recognizing that personality exists in relationship; love begins to define values.

5th Circle—Community & Society

PERSONALITY INTEGRATION: Reason, fairness, and justice mature. Self becomes reliable and trustworthy.
MORALITY FOCUS: Community and society—civic responsibility, cultural participation.
COSMIC RESONANCE: Personality discovers its dignity in service to the whole.

4th Circle—Humanity

PERSONALITY INTEGRATION: Moral and spiritual synthesis; values of compassion and the golden rule govern life.
MORALITY FOCUS: All humanity—identification with the whole human family.
COSMIC RESONANCE: Begins to act as a moral agent for the planet, not just a local circle.

3rd Circle—Universe Citizenship

PERSONALITY INTEGRATION: Soul begins to emerge as a dominant influence.
MORALITY FOCUS: Universe beings—cosmic brotherhood or sisterhood.
COSMIC RESONANCE: Identity enlarges to encompass being a child of God among a vast universe family. A personal seraphic guardian of destiny is assigned.

2nd Circle—The Supreme in Time

PERSONALITY INTEGRATION: Will choices almost completely harmonized with the Adjuster.
MORALITY FOCUS: The evolving Supreme—one's selfhood seen as a part of God's growing finite expression.
COSMIC RESONANCE: Identity now rests in participation with cosmic evolution.

PERSONALITY INTEGRATION: Achieved integration; human will one with divine will; highest attainment in mortal life prior to death.

MORALITY FOCUS: Fusion identity—selfhood anchored in God and in the Supreme.

COSMIC RESONANCE: Identity is now consciously co-creative with God, focused on the divine will.

> *"In the nature of the finaliter is a magnificent universe self, an eternal finaliter son of the Paradise Father as well as the eternal universe child of the Mother Supreme, a universe self qualified to represent both the Father and Mother of universes and personalities in any activity or undertaking pertaining to the finite administration of created, creating, or evolving things and beings."*
> —The Urantia Book, 117:6.7

APPENDIX II:
HOW TO READ
THE URANTIA BOOK

GETTING STARTED

"Are you kidding me—a 2,000 page book with no pictures?" "This book is huge!" "The Foreword is way over my head." "Where do I begin?"

These are common reactions. But if we ease our way into this seemingly formidable tome, we'll soon find that we've discovered a real treasure—an intellectual and spiritual adventure transcending anything we've ever encountered. But nothing ventured, nothing gained—right?

As a starting point, I recommend scanning through the Table of Contents and exploring whatever attracts your interest. Later on, when you've poked around a bit, you'll discover that the Foreword is a valuable reference—almost like an appendix or glossary at the front of the book rather than at the end. Don't get stuck there on your first reading.

Many people start with Part IV due to its narrative flow and its captivating treatment of Jesus. But wherever you start, whatever you explore, there most likely will come a point where you realize it might be fruitful to read it straight through from beginning to end. The key to doing this is the ability to not skip over difficult passages, but to just move on through them, assimilating what you can. Many readers comment on how a passage generated questions in their minds, only to find clarification just a paragraph or two farther into the text.

The narrative is designed by supra-human authors to stimulate your curiosity and to challenge you to engage in creative thing at the frontier of your intellectual and spiritual potentials. S-T-R-E-T-C-H! To take full advantage of this, read prayerfully so that you

47

create engagement with your spiritual benefactors. Invite God into your process.

GETTING SERIOUS

What's the value in reading the text straight through, even if there's much that we struggle to grasp?

The revelators employ the technique of approaching mortal life and our planetary problems by progressing from cosmic abstraction to the most spiritually intimate personal level of daily life. Their strategy is outlined in 19:1.4 through 19:1.12 in The Urantia Book.

Regardless of having been indited by a number of different personalities, the Papers constituting The Urantia Book are not arranged in a random order. They constitute a didactic progression from infinite to local, planetary to personal. By the time we meet Jesus in Part IV, our conceptual scaffolding has been stretched to provide a universe context in which to appreciate the significance of his bestowal, the full scope of divine meaning expressed in a finite life

This is Urantia Book pedagogy. Pedagogy simply means the art or science of teaching—how knowledge, values, or understanding are structured and transmitted so that a learner can grow. Education is what is taught. Pedagogy is how it is taught—the structure, method, sequence, tone, and design that lead to deeper understanding.

In the context of The Urantia Book, when we talk about its pedagogy, we mean its method of revelation: how it builds comprehension step by step—moving from cosmic concepts to local universes, then to planetary history, and finally to a lived example (Jesus). Urantia Book pedagogy is the divine teaching method built into the structure of the revelation itself.;

The revelators of The Urantia Book are intimately familiar with the workings of the mortal mind and its mind/spirit interface. Their pedagogy involves presenting facts in such a manner as to enhance the grasp of meanings and values. Hence the value of following the structure implemented by these master teachers.

48

Architectural Overview: From the Cosmic to the Personal

Part I: The Central and Superuniverses

The text begins at its most abstract level, the nature of Deity, Paradise, and the absolutes. It deliberately stretches our conceptual frame of reference before anything familiar (worlds, souls, or Jesus) appears. This is "universe first" education: It establishes cosmology before theology, ontology before anthropology. *Part I reveals what God is—unity, will, personality, love.*

Part II: The Local Universe

Having defined the macrocosm, it introduces the Creator Son and local universe administration, showing how cosmic principles function within a sub-system of the whole. It's the first step from abstraction of the infinite toward the finite and experiential—the "graduate seminar" version of divine personality and creativity. *Part II shows how Deity creates, governs, and serves.*

Part III: The History of Urantia

Now the focus moves in closer, from universe to planetary. Here human evolution, civilization, and revelation history are placed in context. The pedagogical method is anchoring the universal in the local, giving us a universe frame in which science, anthropology, and religion are integrated, rather than colliding as overlapping domains of inquiry. *Part III shows how divine purpose unf9olds through time.*

Part IV: The Life and Teachings of Jesus

The culminates in narrative, biography; a life story. After three parts of theoretical and cosmic exposition, we meet Jesus as a mortal embodying all the divinity realities outlined in Parts I, II, and III. Every cosmic principle finds its experiential expression in Jesus' choices, goals, purposes, attitudes, relationships, reactions, and teachings. *Part IV reveals divinity in human experience.*

49

In classical pedagogical terms, Part IV is incarnation as demonstration. It turns abstract theology into lived pedagogy—truth made flesh.

Urantia Book pedagogy is the divine teaching method built into the structure of the revelation itself.

THE URANTIA BOOK'S LAYERED STRUCTURE

The conceptual sequence of the Papers is designed to build depth of comprehension. Later statements assume and expand prior definitions, often within the same section of the text. Key ideas recur at multiple scales: personality, mind, love, and purpose are first defined cosmically, then organizationally, then experientially, and finally personally in the life of Jesus. This repetition at descending scales replicates a primary pattern of universe organization.

From Concept to Experience

We are repeatedly moved from intellectual grasp to moral challenge. We don't merely learn facts: We are invited to experience revelation by living truthfully.

The Contrast Method

The narrative continually juxtaposes higher and lower views—evolutionary vs revelatory, material vs spiritual, finite vs eternal—leading us to expand the universe frame within which we are doing our thinking. It leads us to become synthetic thinkers rather than merely analytic collectors of facts; a stimulus to reach out toward the frontier of spiritualized creative imagination.

The Culminating Demonstration

Finally, Part IV exemplifies all previous teaching in one human life. The life of Jesus, the master teacher, is the pedagogical embodiment and demonstration of the cosmology and universe insight outlined in Parts I, II, and III.

This layered structure aims to cultivate cosmic consciousness and spiritual insight—the precursors to the full embrace of cosmic citizenship.

Urantia Book pedagogy moves us from metaphysics to morality, from comprehension to communion, from being curious seekers to becoming co-creators of universe destiny.

So when you're ready to get serious, read it straight through, from beginning to end. And then do it again from time to time as your life unfolds. It will enable your Thought Adjuster to work with you relative to the superadditive entirety of the revelation rather than fragmented parts taken out of context.

Appendix III:
Note on Terminology

This book uses the term "Supreme" in reference to several different aspects of the evolving experiential Deity within which we find ourselves living. This appendix hopefully will serve to provide a basic orientation to meanings implied in the book.

The topic of Supremacy is such an integral part of the revelation that four extensive Papers are devoted to it. A defining overview my be found in Section VII of the Foreword. The Supreme is mentioned over nine hundred times, permeating all four section of The Urantia Book.

THE SUPREME BEING: The Supreme Being is the evolving experiential Deity who is actualizing through the time/space experiences of all finite creatures and Creators. As mortal beings live, choose, and spiritualize their experiences, the Supreme assimilates and integrates the spiritual values and meanings thus produced—the same elements that become part of the evolving mortal soul.

In this way the Supreme harvests the divinely significant values derived from finite evolution—the moral decisions, faith insights, and spiritual attainments of all personal beings—into the growing unity of his own experiential reality. We grow the Supreme as a repercussion of growing our own souls.

GOD THE SUPREME: God the Supreme refers to the full unified and sovereign Deity of the finite, emerging at the culmination of finite evolution at the end of the present universe age. The personality of God the Supreme is currently resident on the Isle of Paradise awaiting the experiential completion of his "body" through the evolution of all finite reality.

THE ALMIGHTY SUPREME: The Almighty Supreme is in process of evolution related to the vast material energies, motions, and cosmic forces of the time/space universes. He is translating the physical evolution of the universes into an ordered, mind managed, purposeful expression of divine will. Upon the completion of the present universe age, the completed Almighty Supreme will unite with the spirit-personality and evolutionary attainments of the Supreme Being, bringing forth the fully actualized God the Supreme, sovereign of the perfected grand universe.

THE SUPREME: When the term "the Supreme" is used in this book, it is a general term referring to the overall phenomenon of Supremacy. It is used as a synonym for "Supremacy."

SUPREMACY: Supremacy is another general term referring to processes related to the evolution of the Supreme Being—experiential Deity.

> *"Mortal man must, through the recognition of truth, the appreciation of beauty, and the worship of goodness, evolve the recognition of a God of love; and then progress through ascending deity levels to the comprehension of the Supreme."*
> —The Urantia Book, 56:6.3

ABOUT THE AUTHOR

David Kantor is a multi-media content creator whose work is dedicated to creating interest in The Urantia Book. A student of the revelation since 1966, he has been involved in the international spread of the book, as well as in the administration of The Urantia Book Fellowship. His work includes two feature length films, books, websites, conference talks and workshops.

A retired software developer from the telecommunications industry, David lives and works in the glorious state of Colorado where he is an active member of Rocky Mountain Spiritual Fellowship.

https://www.urantiabookfilms.org

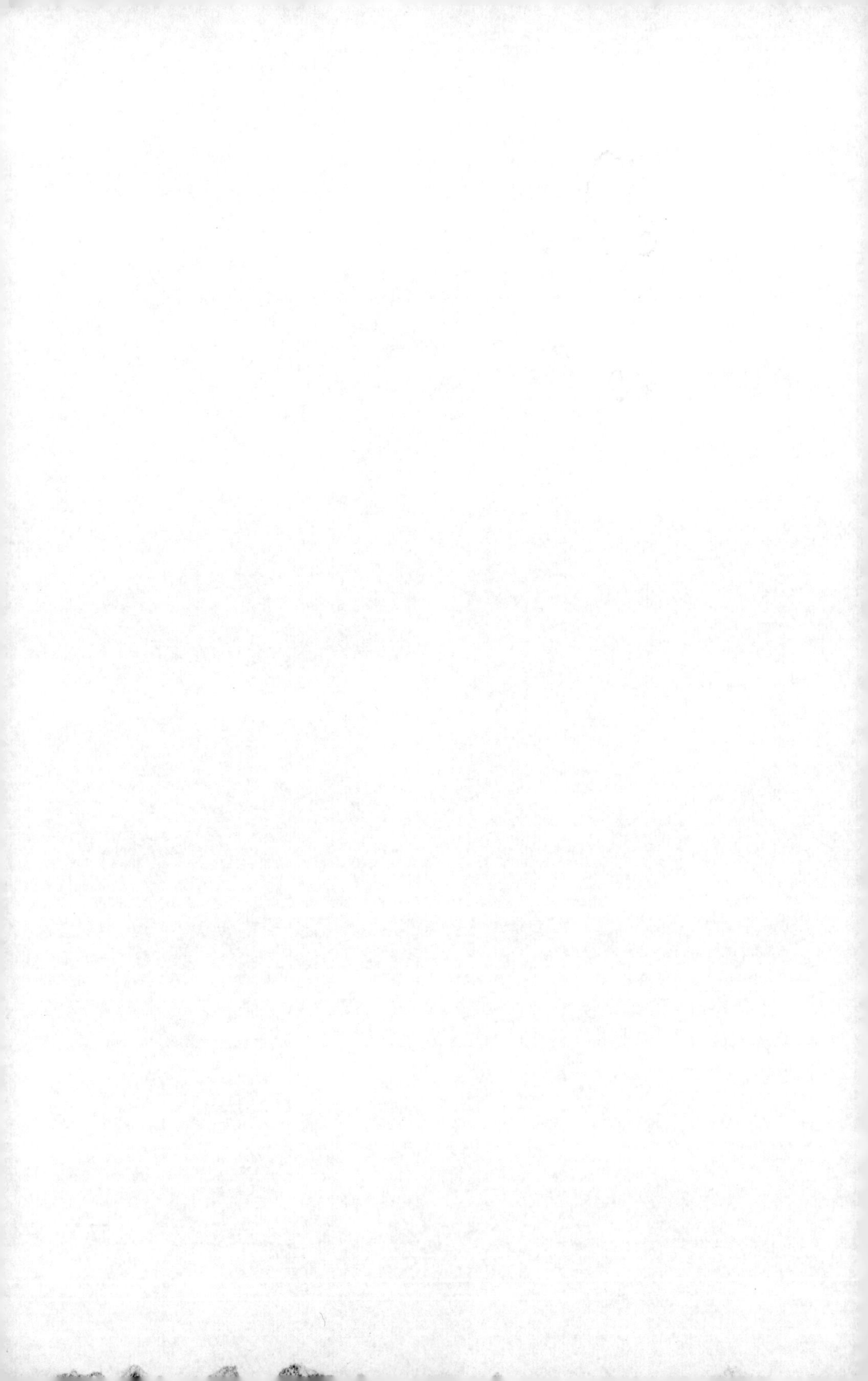

Made in United States
Troutdale, OR
12/21/2025